A PRAYER
for
EVERY CHILD

This edition published by:

Hill of Content Publishing in Australia
hillofcontentpublishing.com
office@hillofcontentpublishing.com
Correspondence: PO Box 24 East Melbourne 8002 Australia
Distribution: 77 Connaught Road Central Hong Kong

Author: Landsman, Gregory
Title: A Prayer for Every Child
Hardcover ISBN: 978-0-6482892-7-2
Design: Louis Romero
1st Edition, 2019

Acknowledgements
I want to thank everyone who contributed to this book, in particularly
my wife. They have helped capture the true spirit and love that children bring.

Ato Aikins; Vinious Armano; Gabriel Braga; Dominic Chung; Patrick Fore; Emma Frances-Logan;
Hal Gatewood; Caroline Hernan; Kat J; Caleb Jones; Wadi Lissa; Omar Lopez; Hanna Morris;
Xavier Mouton; Chi N; Bruno Nascimento; Vishnu Nishad; Mi Pham; Joao Rafael; Andrae Rickett;
Leo Rivas; Maura Silva; Samantha Sophia; Jelleke Vanooteghem; Ben White; Wang Xi; Myung Won
Seo. Siddhant Soni; Avik Saha; Trevor Cole; Nick Karvounis; Sosereybot Kry.

A PRAYER
for
EVERY CHILD

GREGORY LANDSMAN

"I believe in the equality of beauty
That no one is better than who we are
And in the same breath no one is less
In this truth lies our hope, our freedom
And our strength to live a good life."

—— Gregory Landsman

I BELIEVE the mothers and fathers of this and FUTURE generations are our greatest HOPE to create a kinder world and a better FUTURE

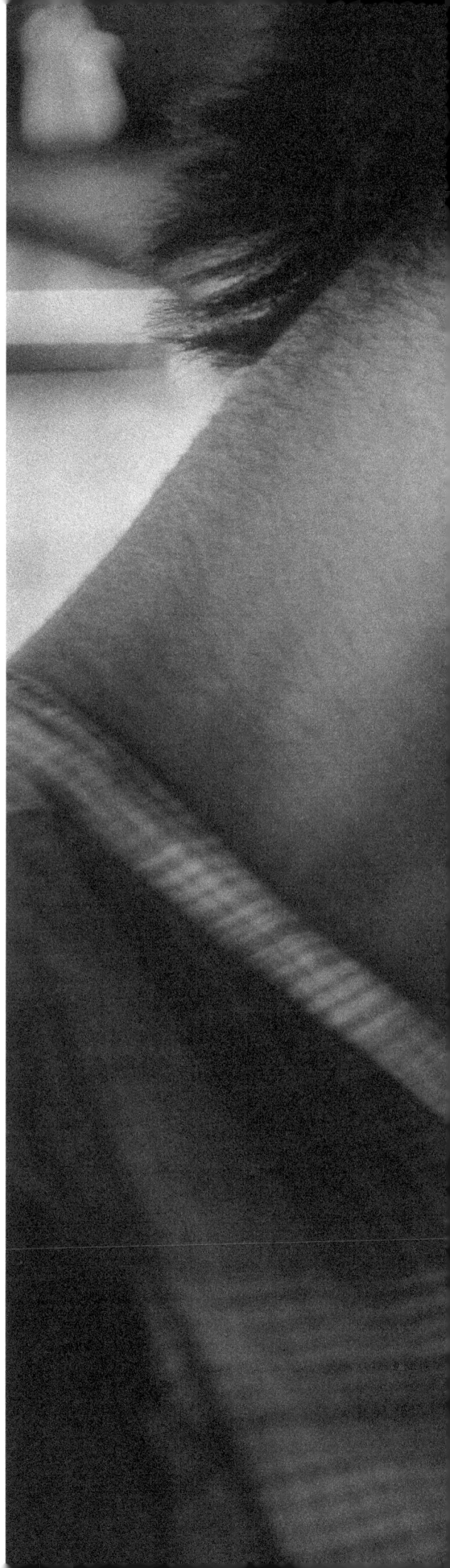

———————

My PRAYER
for every child is...

————

To KNOW they
are supposed to be
DIFFERENT

———

But on the INSIDE
they are all the SAME
———————

To experience the JOY
of friendship and
the hatching of
GREAT plans

———————

But most importantly for EVERY child to play and PLAY

———————

And be a SUPER HERO for the day

———————

A PRAYER FOR EVERY CHILD

To be LOVED like they are the ONLY person in the WORLD

———————

To *EXPRESS*
themselves

———

And SHARE their
SPECIAL gifts

————————

But always SUPPORTED to live their lives in FULL COLOUR

———————

As they LAUGH...

—————

CRY...

_____

A PRAYER FOR EVERY CHILD

*And REACH for
the SKY*

———————

*To be taught that
good FOOD...*

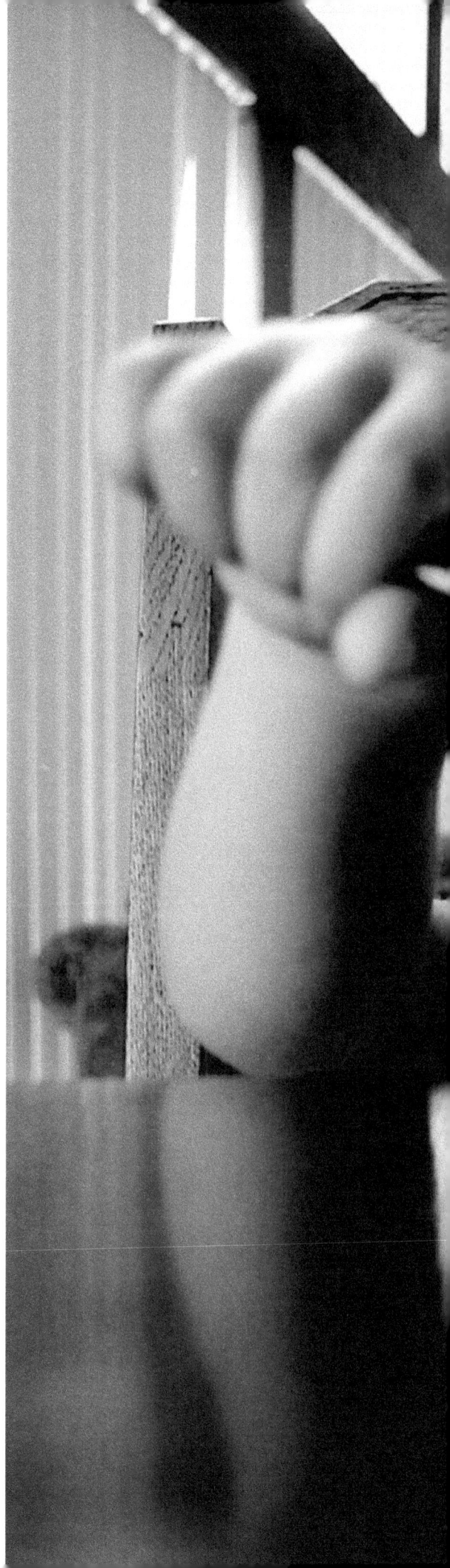

————————

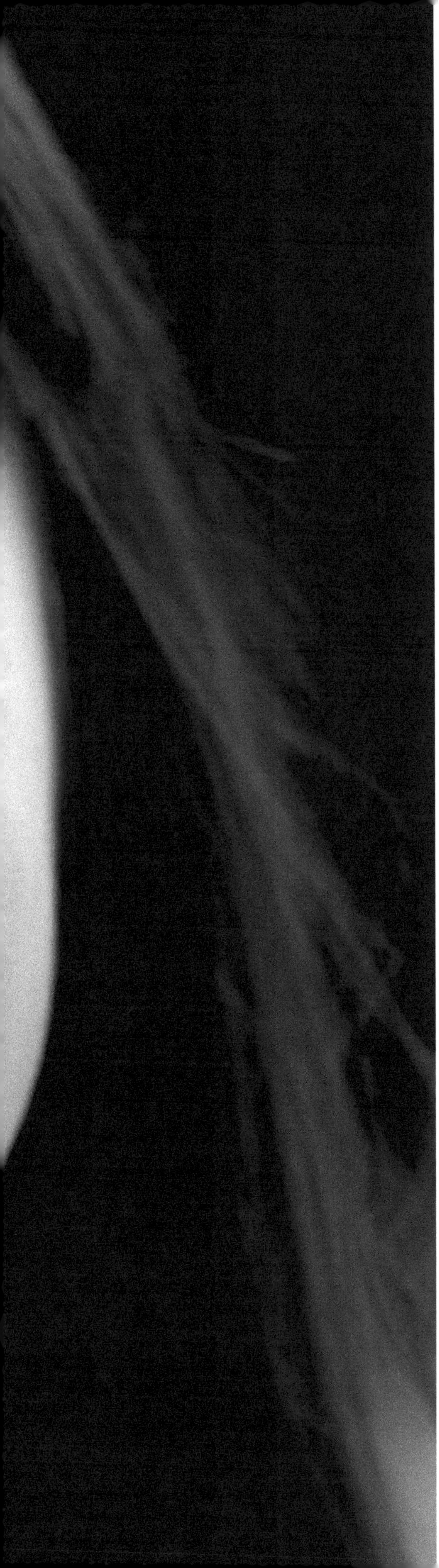

*Equates to good
ENERGY...*

————

*To LIVE a
GOOD life*

———————

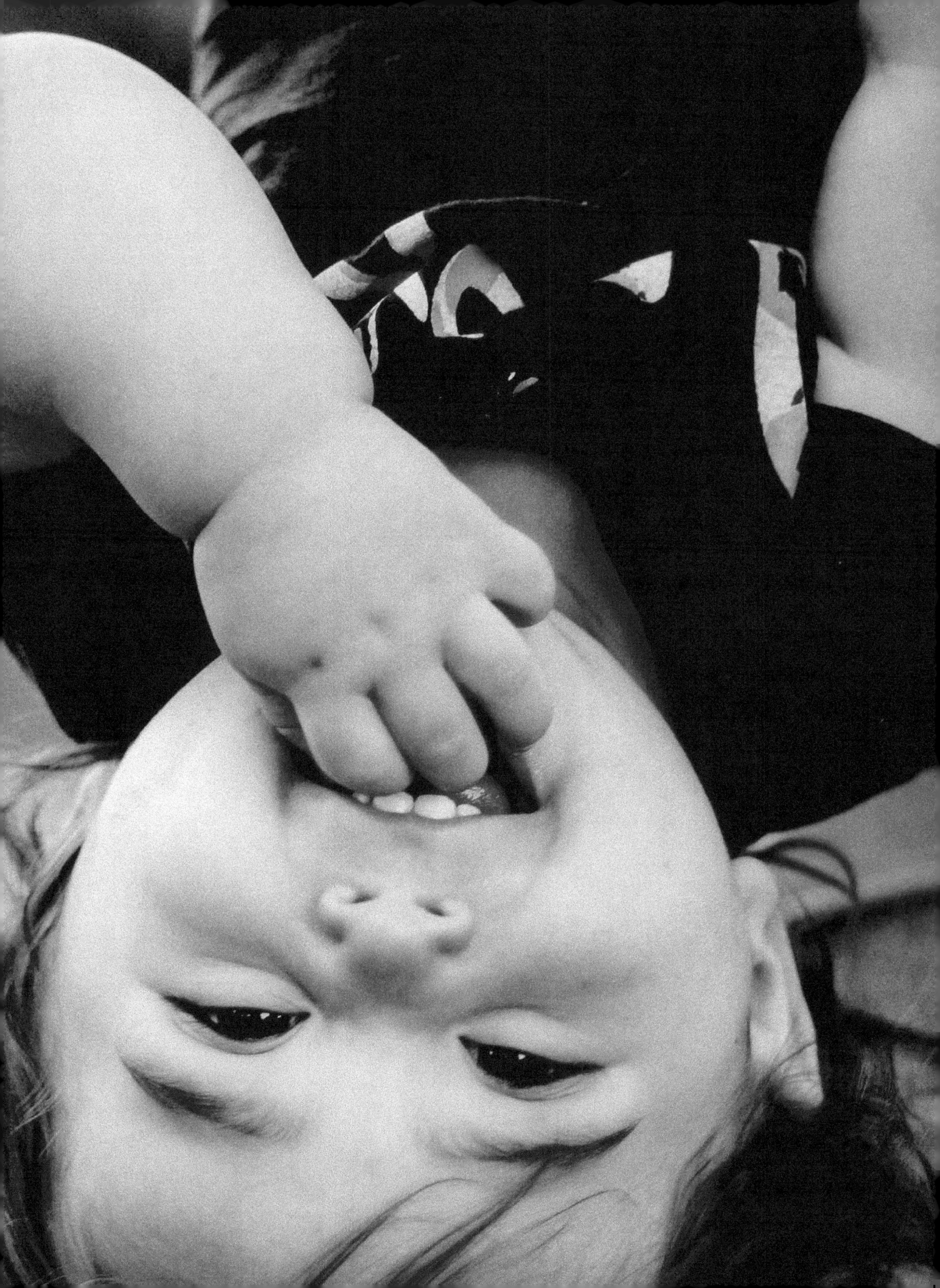

To feel the LOVE of
an ANIMAL

—————

And live JOYFULLY
with NATURE

———————

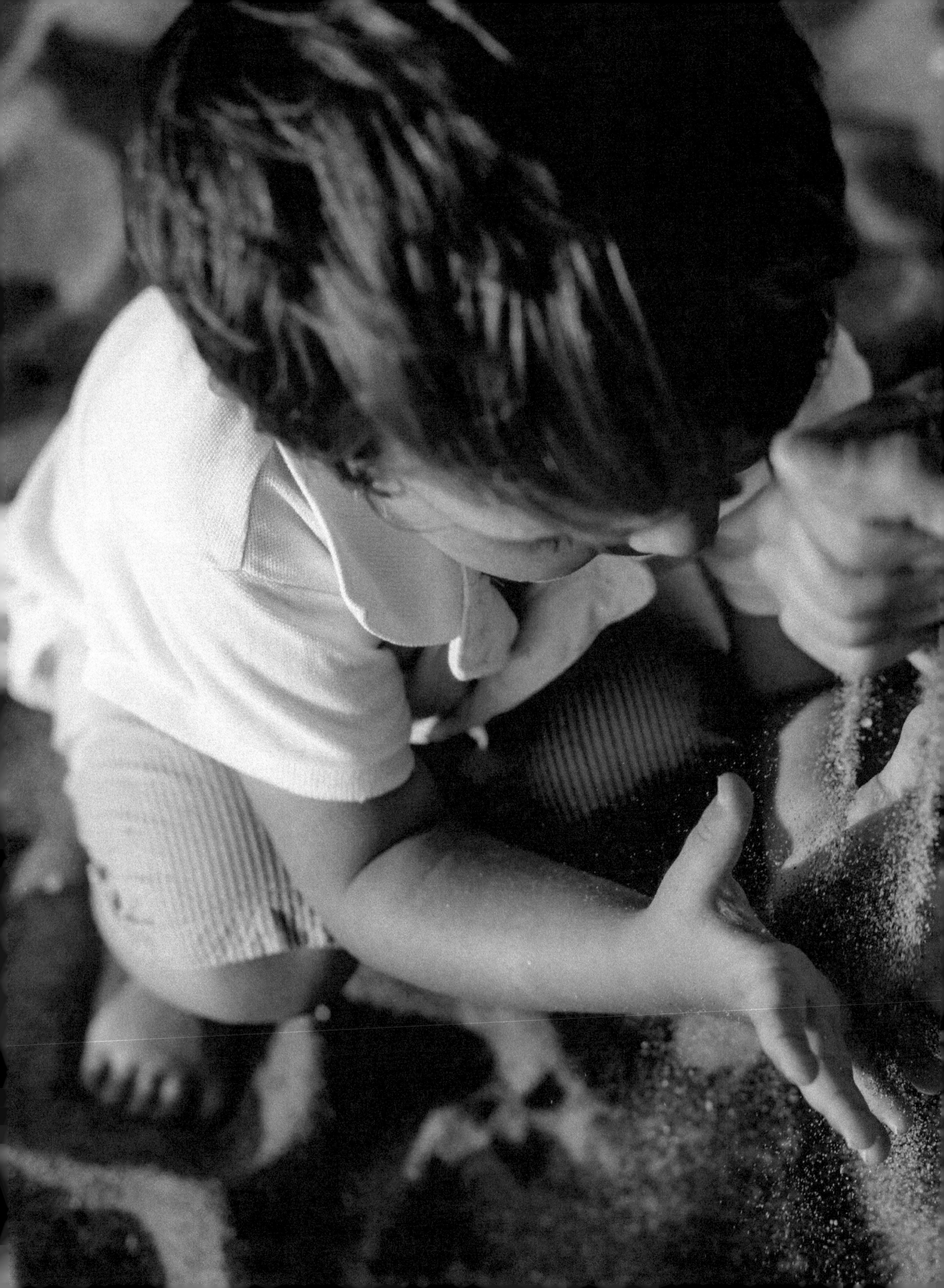

But always allowed
the PLEASURE of
sand between
their TOES

———————

And getting DIRT on their CLOTHES

————————

A PRAYER FOR EVERY CHILD

To live daily with the COMFORT of deep SLEEP and a peaceful HEART

To enjoy a LIFE that knows the VALUE of KINDNESS and RESPECT

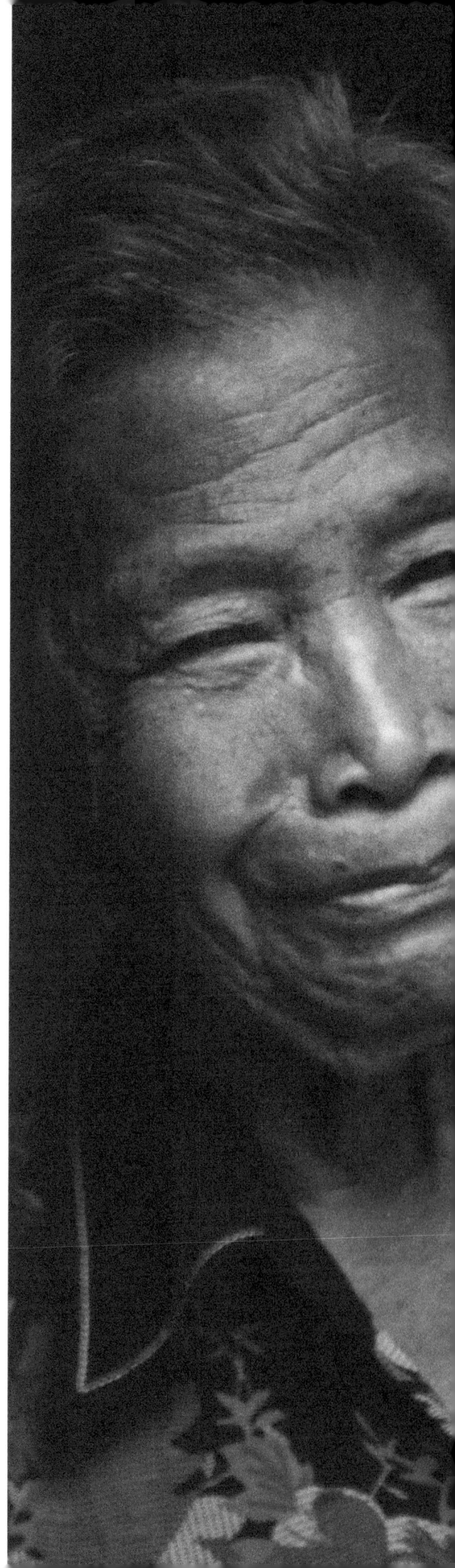

———

A PRAYER FOR EVERY CHILD

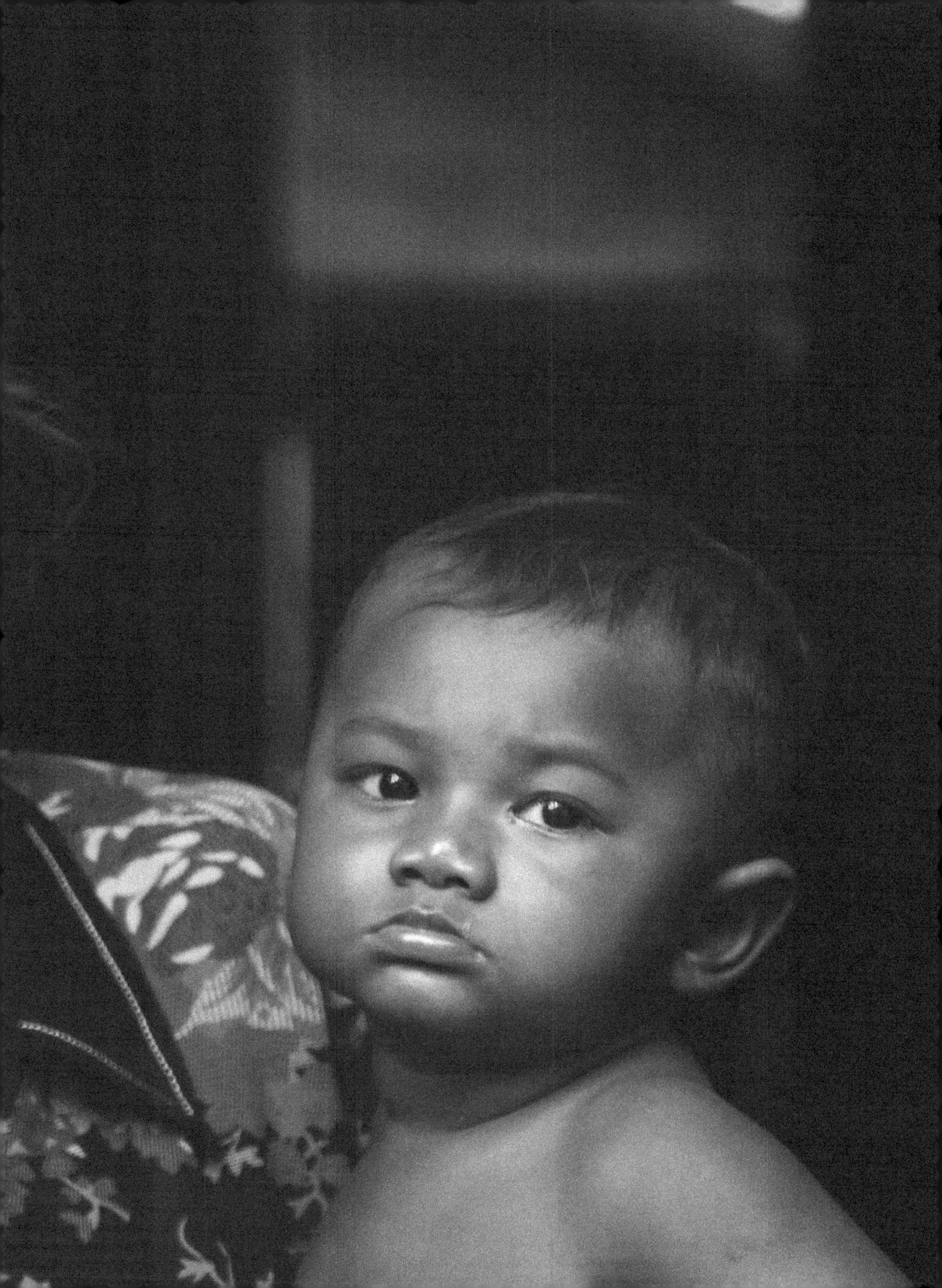

And though they are
SMALL…

————————

*Let them know
that SIZE is an
ATTITUDE so they'll
be 100 FEET tall*

———————

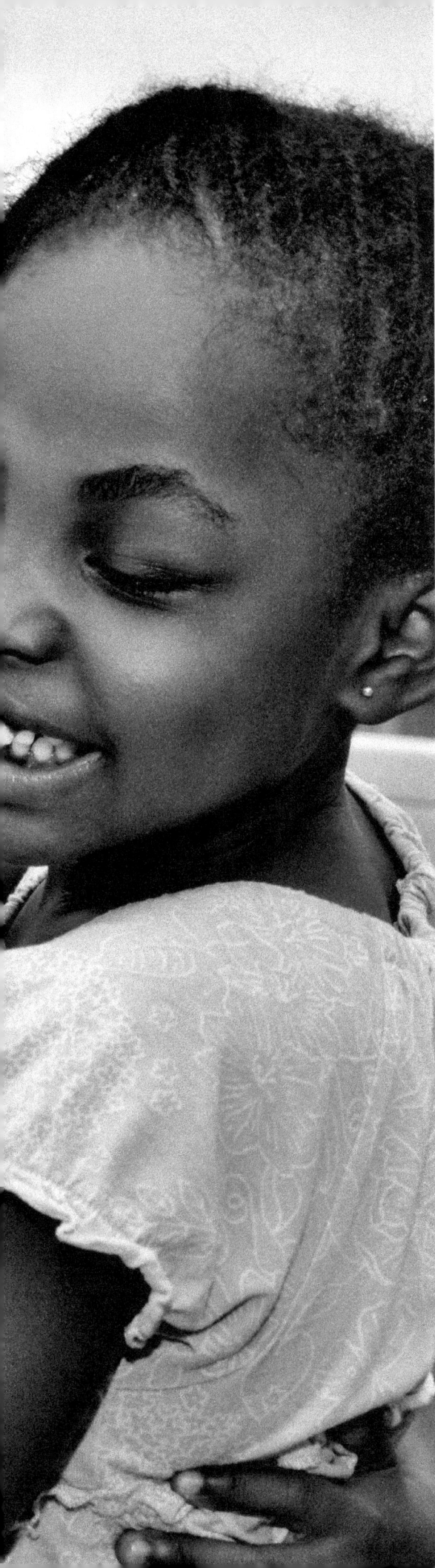

To believe that
WINNING isn't
as important as
SHARING and
JOINING in

————————

*To feel CONFIDENT
walking their
OWN path*

———————

*Because SOMEONE
has their BACK*

———————

*Granting EVERY
parents GREATEST
wish*

———————

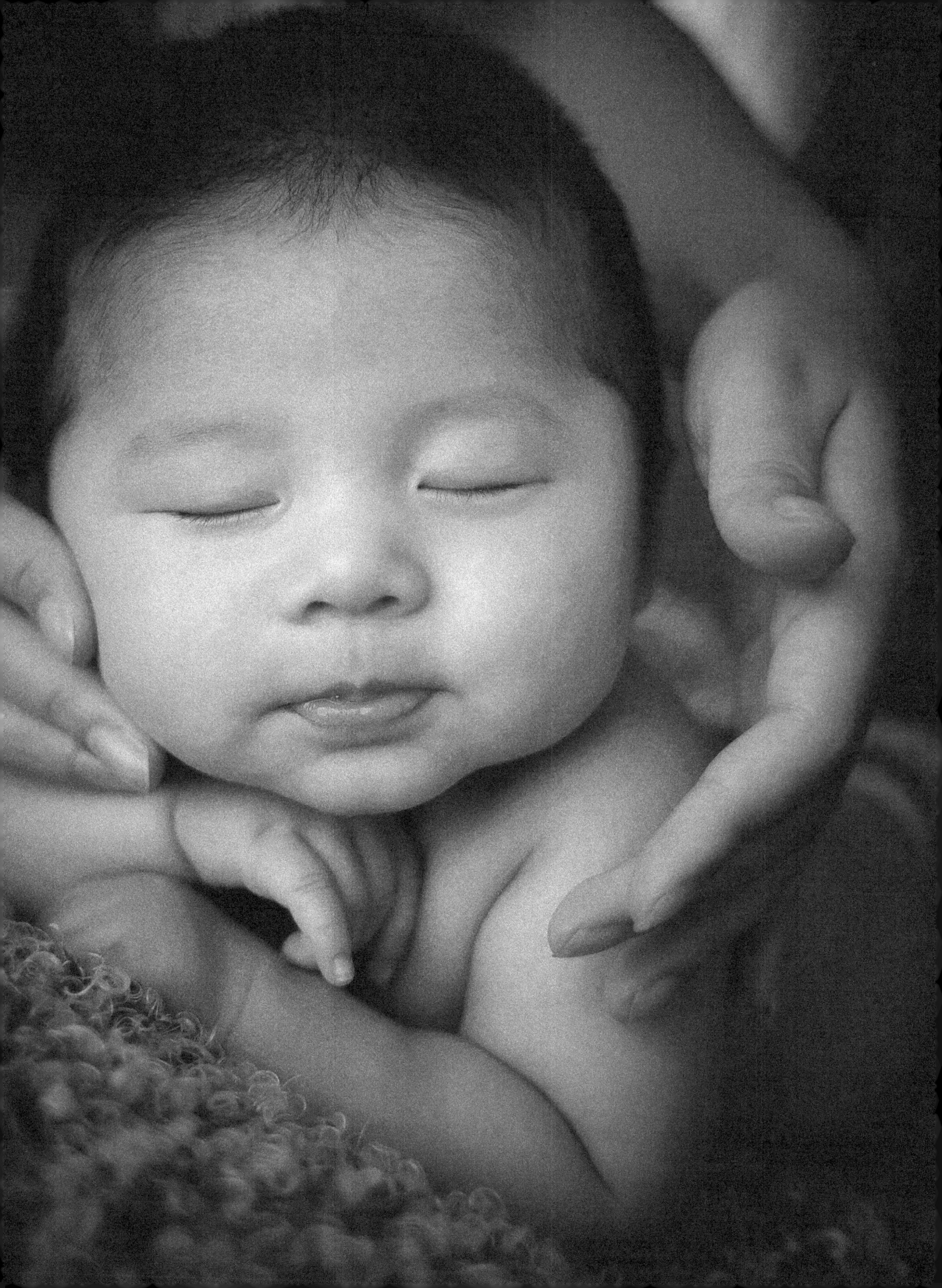

That they'll be the BEST they can BE…

———————

And live FOREVER
FREE...

————

A PRAYER FOR EVERY CHILD

A PRAYER FOR EVERY CHILD

I believe the mothers and fathers of this and future generations are our
greatest hope to create a kinder world and a better future.

My prayer for every child is:

To know they are supposed to be different, but on the inside they are
all the same
To experience the joy of friendship and the hatching of great plans
But most importantly for every child to play and play, and be a super hero
for the day.

To be loved like they are the only person in the world
To express themselves and celebrate their special gifts
But always supported to live their lives in full colour as they laugh,
cry and reach for the sky.

To be taught that good food equates to good energy, to live a good life
To feel the love of an animal and live joyfully with nature
But always allowed the pleasure of sand between their toes and getting dirt
on their clothes.

To live daily with the comfort of deep sleep and a peaceful heart
To enjoy a life that knows the value of kindness and respect
And though they are small, let them know that size is an attitude so they'll
be 100 feet tall.

To believe that winning isn't as important as sharing and joining in
To feel confident walking their own path, because someone has their back
Granting every parents greatest wish, that they'll be the best they can be and
live forever free.

Gregory Landsman

ABOUT THE AUTHOR

Gregory Landsman is a best selling author of nine books on inner and outer beauty.

Having grown up in South Africa under the Apartheid system, Gregory's early years were marked by daily beatings, bullying and rejection.

Gregory turned his pain into success through a thirty-year career in the global beauty industry, discovering through the extremes of his life experience, his own transformational BEAUTY philosophy that underpins his books and courses, and is shared with the many thousands of people he engages with each year through TV, speaking appearances and media.

Gregory is the CEO of the GL Skinfit Institute, an organisation that promotes and upholds the values of inclusion, diversity, individuality, respect, kindness, compassion, collaboration, acceptance and self discovery. Its vision is a world where differences are not merely tolerated but embraced and celebrated.

Gregory is an expert commentator on beauty, wellness and body image. As an inspirational speaker, his personal journey delivers an empowering message about overcoming tragedy and adversity through the power of self-belief. His story of beating the odds is motivating and uplifting, reminding people that life is not about limitations, but endless possibilities.

Gregory is also the host of the global television show *Face Lifting Food*, based on two of his books (FACE FOOD & FACE VALUE), about how to cook your way to healthier, brighter, younger looking skin.

BOOKS BY AUTHOR

A Lifetime of Beauty
Faith Lifting Prayers
Face Value
Face Fitness
Face Food
Face Secrets
The Balance of Beauty Explodes the Body Myth
Stop Stress Fast

www.ingramcontent.com/pod-product-compliance
Lightning Source LLC
Chambersburg PA
CBHW040301100426

42811CB00011B/1333